T0061166

Symbols of
FREEDOM

PIONEER EDITION

By Frank Mills and Meg Runyan

CONTENTS

The Face o

f Freedom

The Statue of Liberty has welcomed immigrants to the United States for over one hundred years. Pay a visit to Lady Liberty. Find out why she's a universal symbol of freedom and democracy.

By Frank Mills
Deputy Superintendent
Statue of Liberty National Monument

Perfect Spot. *Artist Frédéric-Auguste Bartholdi picked this island in New York Harbor for his famous statue.*

live at the Statue of Liberty. How cool is that? After all, she is a popular sight. Thousands of people visit her each day. My job is looking after her. I take great pride in that.

Lady Liberty stands for the right to be free. France gave her to us as a gift of friendship. She was opened in October 1886. Join me on Liberty Island for a closer look at this beloved American symbol.

Meet Lady Liberty

Imagine visiting the statue. To get here, you take a boat. You board in New York or New Jersey. After you land, you walk up to the statue.

You have to lean back and look up to see the statue. Lady Liberty is 46 meters (151 feet) tall. That is not counting the base. She is Earth's largest metal statue.

Look at her left hand. It holds a tablet. On it is a date: July 4, 1776. That is the birthday of the United States. Her right arm holds up a flame. It **represents**, or stands for, the light of freedom.

On her head, she wears a big crown. It has seven rays. They stand for **liberty** shining on the seven continents. Below her feet is a broken chain. It shows we are free.

The Statue's Story

Lady Liberty is huge. Her shoe size is 879! Making her took a lot of copper. Workers in France pounded the copper with hammers. The metal is as thick as two pennies. People paid to watch the work.

Workers then packed Liberty's parts into crates. They came to the United States on a ship. Americans gave money to build a base for the statue. Kids gave some money, too.

Building Liberty was like a puzzle. That is because some pieces were marked wrong! Putting the statue together took months.

Old Metal, New Meanings

Over time, people saw Lady Liberty in new ways. Millions of people moved to America. Many came to New York by ship. Lady Liberty welcomed them. To them, she stood for hope. They saw a new life in a new land.

In 2001, people saw something else. We were attacked on September 11th. The statue gave comfort to people. She seemed to say we were still free. Visitors got the message, and their tears became smiles. That is the power of Lady Liberty!

Making Liberty. *This painting shows the Staue of Liberty in Paris, France. That is where she was made.*

Wordwise

liberty: the freedom to live the way you want to

represent: is a sign or symbol of something

JOURNEY TO
America's Capital

Washington, D.C., lies about 230 miles south of the Statue of Liberty. It's the nation's capital. And like Lady Liberty, it inspires people.

About 16 million people visit each year! Most head toward places shown on this map. If you visited the city, what places would you want to see?

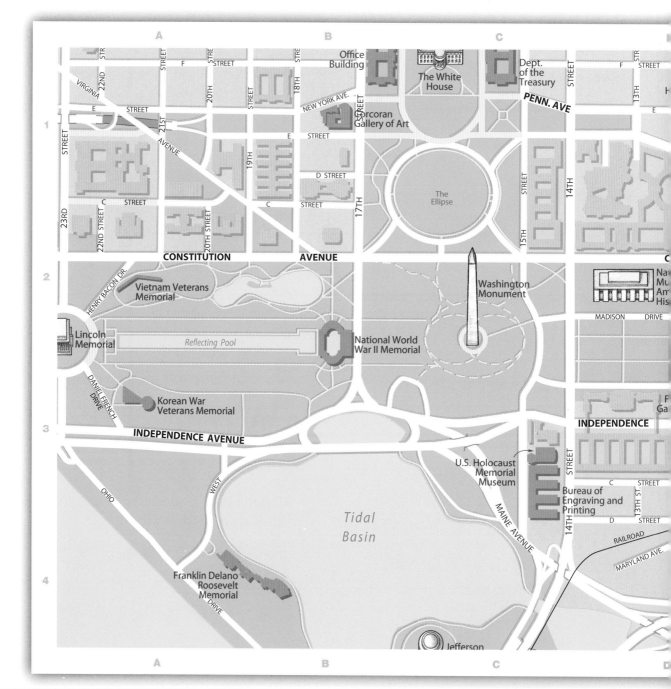

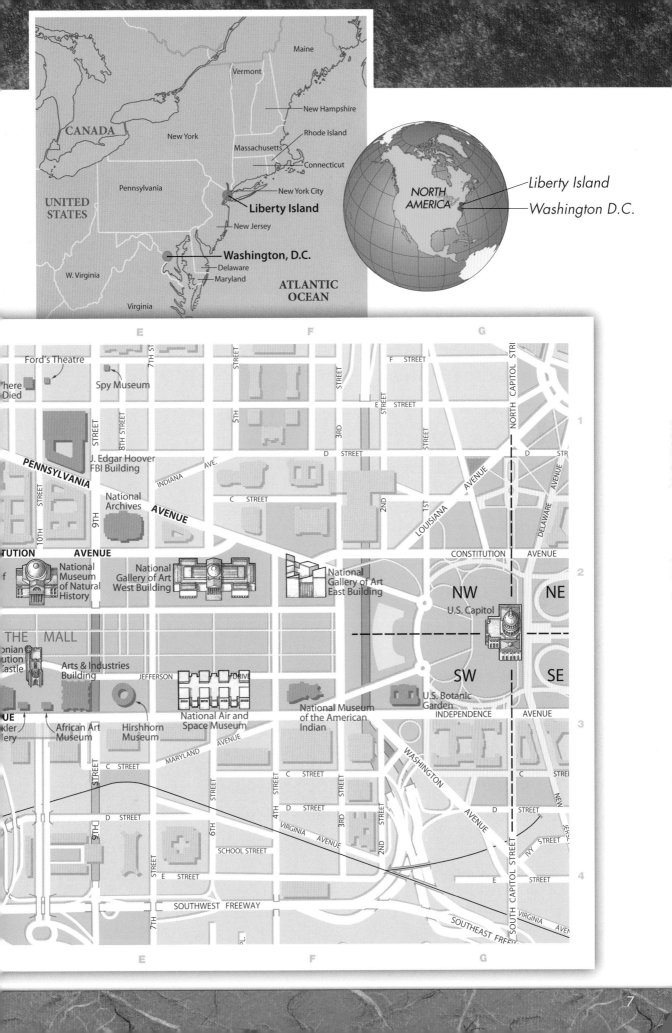

Maine

Vermont

New Hampshire

CANADA

New York

Rhode Island

Massachusetts

Connecticut

Pennsylvania

New York City

Liberty Island

UNITED
STATES

New Jersey

W. Virginia

Washington, D.C.

Delaware

Maryland

Virginia

ATLANTIC
OCEAN

NORTH
AMERICA

Liberty Island

Washington D.C.

Ford's Theatre

here
Died

Spy Museum

7TH ST

STREET

F STREET

STREET

NORTH CAPITOL STR

5TH

3RD

E STREET

STREET

8TH STREET

STREET

D STREET

PENNSYLVANIA

J. Edgar Hoover
FBI Building

INDIANA

AVE.

D STR

AVENUE

DELAWARE AVENUE

National
Archives

AVENUE

C STREET

2ND

LOUISIANA

STREET

1ST

9TH STREET

10TH STREET

CONSTITUTION AVENUE

TUTION AVENUE

National
Museum
of Natural
History

National
Gallery of Art
West Building

National
Gallery of Art
East Building

CONSTITUTION AVENUE

NW

NE

U.S. Capitol

THE MALL

onian
ution
astle

Arts & Industries
Building

JEFFERSON

DRIVE

SW

SE

UE

kler
ery

African Art
Museum

Hirshhorn
Museum

National Air and
Space Museum

National Museum
of the American
Indian

U.S. Botanic
Garden

INDEPENDENCE AVENUE

WASHINGTON

MARYLAND AVENUE

C STREET

C STREET

9TH STREET

D STREET

4TH STREET

D STREET

6TH STREET

VIRGINIA AVENUE

3RD STREET

2ND STREET

AVENUE

D STREET

NEW

E STREET

SCHOOL STREET

SOUTH CAPITOL STREET

IVY STREET

E STREET

VIRGINIA AVEN

7TH

SOUTHWEST FREEWAY

SOUTHEAST FREE

Exploring Washington, D.C.

By Meg Runyan

For centuries, people have come to the United States to find a new kind of government. Kid explorer Meg Runyan spent three busy days in Washington, D.C.—the center of that government. Follow along as she gives you a kid's-eye view of our nation's capital.

Invitation to Adventure

I had the opportunity to spend three days in Washington, D.C. The trip was an amazing adventure into history. Here are some highlights from my trip.

The Heart of Town

Washington, D. C. has many important places, but the Capitol is the center of town.

The first thing I noticed about the Capitol was its big white dome. The dome is made of iron. It weighs about nine million pounds!

Beneath the dome is a large circular room called the Rotunda. It is decorated with paintings and statues honoring famous Americans.

U.S. Capitol

Lawmakers

All those statues and paintings are cool. But they are not why the Capitol matters. The famous building is home to Congress. This is the branch of government that makes America's laws.

Congress has two parts. The Senate has 100 members. The House of Representatives has over 400 members.

Senators and representatives have hard jobs. They help make the laws that everyone follows in the United States. A law starts out as a **bill**. If at least half of Congress approves it, the bill goes the President.

The President may approve the bill. If that happens, it becomes a law. The President may also reject, or **veto**, it. If that happens, Congress can vote on it again. If two-thirds of Congress approves it, then the bill becomes a law.

Meg visits former Senator Jeffords.

Washington Monument

The Gentleman From Vermont

While I was at the Capitol, I met former Senator Jim Jeffords from Vermont. His goal is "to make sure the U.S. does its best" for its people. Jeffords wants all kids to get a good education. He also believes deeply in protecting our environment.

Making laws isn't easy. Lawmakers have different ideas about what America needs. It takes a lot of work and patience to get them to agree.

At times, Jeffords got discouraged. Then he looked out his office window. Seeing the Capitol dome always **inspired** the senator. It reminded him that we can get things done.

A Day with the Presidents

Washington is a great place to learn about our Presidents. **Monuments** help visitors to remember our important leaders.

First, I visited the Franklin Delano Roosevelt Memorial. Then I decided to rent a paddleboat.

From the water, I got a great view of the Jefferson Memorial. He was our third President. He was also the main author of the Declaration of Independence.

I also saw the Washington Monument. It rises above the city. George Washington was our first President. He also decided where the capital city should be built.

Jefferson Memorial

The White House at night

Lincoln Memorial

The President's House

My next stop was the White House. It has been the home of our President since 1800.

The White House has been through many changes over the years. The biggest change happened during the War of 1812 when America and England were fighting. In August 1814, British forces invaded Washington, D.C. The President and his wife fled. Then British troops burned the White House.

Afterward, the White House had to be almost completely rebuilt. The work was not finished until September 1817.

It's Over Already?!

My three days in Washington, D.C. passed too quickly. I wish I had more time to explore! Still my trip gave me a better understanding of our government and how it works. It also made me **proud** to be part of this great country.

Wordwise

bill: proposed law

inspire: to cause someone to have a positive feeling or emotion

monument: structure built so people remember a person or event

proud: showing self-respect

veto: reject a proposed law

Built to Inspire

Find out about U.S. monuments. Then answer these questions.

1 How did the United States get the Statue of Liberty? What does her crown represent?

2 Describe two meanings people attach to the Statue of Liberty.

3 The President of the United States can veto laws. What does *veto* mean?

4 What does Meg Runyan learn from her visit to Washington, D.C.?

5 How are the Statue of Liberty and Washington, D.C., similar? How are they different?